The Picture of Dorian Gray

OSCAR WILDE

Level 4

Retold by Kieran McGovern
Series Editors: Andy Hopkins and Jocelyn Potter

D1563073

Pearson Education Limited
Edinburgh Gate, Harlow,
Essex CM20 2JE, England
and Associated Companies throughout the world.

ISBN-13: 978-0-582-41808-0
ISBN-10: 0-582-41808-9

The Picture of Dorian Gray was first published in complete book form in 1891
This adaptation first published by Penguin Books 1994
Published by Addison Wesley Longman Limited and Penguin Books Ltd. 1998
New edition first published 1999

10

Text copyright © Kieran McGovern 1994
Illustrations copyright © David Cuzik 1994
All rights reserved

The moral right of the adapter and of the illustrator has been asserted

Typeset by RefineCatch Limited, Bungay, Suffolk
Set in 11/14pt Monotype Bembo
Printed in China
SWTC/10

Published by Pearson Education Limited in association with
Penguin Books Ltd, both companies being subsidiaries of Pearson Plc

For a complete list of titles available in the Penguin Readers series please write to your local
Pearson Education office or contact: Penguin Readers Marketing Department,
Pearson Education, Edinburgh Gate, Harlow, Essex, CM20 2JE.

Contents

Introduction

If I could stay young and the picture grow old! For that – for that – I would give everything. I would give my soul for that!

When Basil Hallward paints a picture of the young and handsome Dorian Gray, he thinks it is the most important work of his life. But he cannot guess how important it will be to Dorian Gray himself. Because when Dorian sees the finished portrait, he makes a terrible wish: that the beautiful young man in the picture in front of him will grow old and that he will look young for ever. Unfortunately for Dorian, and everyone he knows, his wish comes true – in a most terrible way . . .

One of the most important Irish writers of the nineteenth century, Oscar Wilde was born in Dublin, Ireland, in 1854. His father was a doctor and his mother a writer and translator. He went to Dublin and Oxford Universities, where he was an unusually clever student. At Oxford he won an important prize but he was even more famous for his unusual personal style. His long hair, bright clothes, amusing conversation and ideas about art won him many followers. His habit of making fun of people also won him enemies.

His first book of poems appeared in 1881 but it did not bring him much money. He went on a tour of the United States, where he gave talks on art and society.

In 1884 Wilde married Constance Lloyd, and they decided to live in London. Constance later gave birth to two sons, Cyril and Vyvyan.

Wilde began to work seriously at his writing in 1887, beginning with a story, *The Canterville Ghost*. He wrote many other stories, among them *The Picture of Dorian Gray* (1892). He also wrote plays about fashionable society, including *Lady Windermere's Fan* (1892),

A Woman of No Importance (1893) and *An Ideal Husband* (1895). Most popular of all was *The Importance of Being Earnest*, which many people think is one of the funniest plays ever written in English. Wilde also wrote a play in French, *Salomé* (1893), which takes the story of King Herod's daughter from the Bible.

But in 1895 everything changed and Oscar Wilde's success in public life was over. Wilde had become a close friend of Lord Alfred Douglas, a young man from a wealthy family. Douglas's father, the Marquess of Queensberry, found some letters from Wilde to Douglas and realized that the two men were lovers. He did everything he could to ruin Wilde. Three court cases followed, and they received much publicity in the national newspapers. Douglas escaped any kind of punishment but Wilde was sent to prison for two years. After this many of his friends turned their backs on him and nobody was willing to put on his plays.

Wilde suffered terribly during his time in prison. He became ill and his confidence, both as a person and an artist, was destroyed. At first he was not allowed to do any writing but later he produced a long poem called *The Ballad of Reading Gaol*. It describes the crime of a poor soldier and the cruelty of life in prison. When the poem appeared in 1898, it was a best-seller.

In 1897, when Wilde came out of prison, he was a broken man. He wanted to go back to his wife but she refused to have him, although she did give him some money to live on. It was impossible for him to live in England, so he lived for a time in northern France. A few loyal friends visited him there. He managed to spend a few months with Douglas, against the wishes of both families, but soon they had no money: neither had ever learned how to live cheaply. Wilde spent the last years of his life in Paris, living in cheap hotels and asking his friends for money. During the years after leaving prison, he produced no literary work. He died in November 1900, at the age of forty-six.

♦

Today Oscar Wilde's sexual behaviour is no longer criticized as it was in his lifetime. Instead, he is remembered for his writings and for his daring ideas. As a thinker, he believed strongly in the value of beauty, in life as well as in art, although *The Picture of Dorian Gray* shows the dangers of such beliefs. Wilde is admired for his imaginative stories, plays and humorous sayings, which both shocked and entertained people.

Chapter 1   An Extraordinarily Beautiful Young Man

The room was filled with the smell of roses. Sitting on a sofa, smoking a cigarette, was Lord Henry Wotton. Through the open door came the distant sounds of the London streets.

In the centre of the room stood a portrait of an extraordinarily beautiful young man. Sitting a little distance in front of it was the artist himself, Basil Hallward. As the painter looked at the portrait, he smiled.

'It is your best work, Basil, the best thing you have ever done,' said Lord Henry, slowly. 'You really must send it next year to the Grosvenor. The Grosvenor is really the only place to exhibit a painting like that.'

'I don't think I shall send it anywhere,' the painter answered, moving his head in that odd way that used to make his friends laugh at him at Oxford University. 'No: I won't send it anywhere.'

Lord Henry looked at him in surprise through the thin blue smoke of his cigarette. 'Not send it anywhere? My dear man, why not? What odd people you painters are!'

'I know you will laugh at me,' Basil replied, 'but I really can't exhibit it. I have put too much of myself into it.'

Lord Henry stretched himself out on the sofa and laughed. 'Too much of yourself in it! Basil, this man is truly beautiful. He does not look like you.'

'You don't understand me, Harry,' answered the artist. 'Of course I am not like him. I would be sorry to look like him. It is better not to be different from other people. The stupid and ugly have the best of this world. Dorian Gray – '

'Dorian Gray? Is that his name?' asked Lord Henry, walking across the room towards Basil Hallward.

'Yes, that is his name. I wasn't going to tell you.'

'But why not?'

'Oh, I can't explain. When I like people enormously I never tell their names to anyone. I suppose you think that's very foolish?'

'Not at all,' answered Lord Henry, 'not at all, my dear Basil. You forget that I am married so my life is full of secrets. I never know where my wife is, and my wife never knows what I am doing. When we meet we tell each other lies with the most serious faces.'

'I hate the way you talk about your married life, Harry,' said Basil Hallward, walking towards the door that led into the garden. 'I believe you are really a very good husband, but that you are ashamed of it. You never say a good thing, and you never do a wrong thing.'

Lord Henry laughed and the two men went out into the garden together. After a pause, Lord Henry pulled out his watch. 'I am afraid I have to go, Basil,' he said in a quiet voice. 'But before I go I want you to explain to me why you won't exhibit Dorian Gray's picture. I want the real reason.'

'I told you the real reason.'

'No, you did not. You said that it was because there was too much of yourself in it. Now, that is childish.'

'Harry,' said Basil Hallward, looking him straight in the face, 'every portrait that is painted with feeling is a portrait of the artist, not the sitter. I will not exhibit this picture because I am afraid that I have shown in it the secret of my own soul.'

Lord Henry laughed. 'And what is that?' he asked.

'Oh, there is really very little to tell, Harry,' answered the painter, 'and I don't think you will understand. Perhaps you won't believe it.'

Lord Henry smiled and picked a flower from the grass. 'I am quite sure I'll understand it,' he replied, staring at the flower, 'and I can believe anything.'

'The story is simply this,' said the painter. 'Two months ago I went to a party at Lady Brandon's. After I had been in the room for about ten minutes, I suddenly realized that someone was looking at me. I turned around and saw Dorian Gray for the first time. When our eyes met, I felt the blood leaving my face. I knew that this boy would become my whole soul, my whole art itself.'

'What did you do?'

'We were quite close, almost touching. Our eyes met again. I asked Lady Brandon to introduce me to him.'

'What did Lady Brandon say about Mr Dorian Gray?'

'Oh, something like "Charming boy. I don't know what he does – I think he doesn't do anything. Oh, yes, he plays the piano – or is it the violin, dear Mr Gray?" Dorian and I both laughed and we became friends at once.'

'Laughter is not at all a bad beginning for a friendship,' said the young lord, picking another flower, 'and it is the best ending for one.'

Hallward shook his head. 'You don't understand what friendship is, Harry. Everyone is the same to you.'

'That's not true!' cried Lord Henry, pushing his hat back, and looking at the summer sky. 'I choose my friends for their beauty and my enemies for their intelligence. A man cannot be too careful in choosing his enemies. Of course, I hate my relations. And I hate poor people because they are ugly, stupid and drunk –'

'I don't agree with a word you have said. And I feel sure that you don't agree either.'

Lord Henry touched his pointed brown beard with his finger, and the toe of his boot with his stick. 'How English you are, Basil! An Englishman is only interested in whether he agrees with an idea, not whether it is right or wrong. But tell me more about Mr Dorian Gray. How often do you see him?'

'Every day. I couldn't be happy if I didn't see him every day.'

'How extraordinary! I thought you only cared about your art.'

'He is all my art to me now,' said the painter. 'I know that the work I have done since I met Dorian Gray is the best work of my life. In some strange way his personality has shown me a new kind of art. He seems like a little boy – though he is really more than twenty – and when he is with me I see the world differently.'

'Basil, this is extraordinary! I must see Dorian Gray.'

Hallward got up from his seat and walked up and down the garden. After some time he came back. 'Harry,' he said. 'Dorian Gray is the reason for my art. You might see nothing in him. I see everything in him.'

'Then why won't you exhibit his portrait?' asked Lord Henry.

'An artist should paint beautiful things, but he should put nothing of his own life into them. Some day I will show the world what that beauty is. For that reason the world will never see my portrait of Dorian Gray.'

'I think you are wrong, Basil, but I won't argue with you. Tell me, is Dorian Gray very fond of you?'

The painter thought for a few moments. 'He likes me,' he answered, after a pause. 'I know he likes me. Of course I flatter him too much and tell him things that I should not. He is usually very charming to me, and we spend thousands of wonderful hours together. But sometimes he can be horribly thoughtless and seems to enjoy causing me pain. Then I feel, Harry, that I have given my whole soul to someone who uses it like a flower to put in his coat on a summer's day.'

'Summer days are long, Basil,' said Lord Henry in a quiet voice. 'Perhaps you will get bored before he will. Intelligence lives longer than beauty. One day you will look at your friend and you won't like his colour or something. And then you will begin to think that he has behaved badly towards you –'

'Harry, don't talk like that. As long as I live, Dorian Gray will be everything to me. You can't feel what I feel. You change too often.'

'My dear Basil, that is exactly why I can feel it.' Lord Henry took a cigarette from his pretty silver box and lit it. Then he turned to Hallward and said, 'I have just remembered.'

4

'Remembered what, Harry?'

'Where I heard the name of Dorian Gray.'

'Where was it?' asked Hallward with a frown.

'Don't look so angry, Basil. It was at my aunt's, Lady Agatha's. She told me that she had discovered this wonderful young man. He was going to help her work with the poor people in the East End of London, and his name was Dorian Gray. Of course I didn't know it was your friend.'

'I am very glad you didn't, Harry.'

'Why?'

'I don't want you to meet him.'

A servant came into the garden. 'Mr Dorian Gray is waiting in the house, sir,' he said.

'You must introduce me now,' cried Lord Henry, laughing.

The painter turned to his servant. 'Ask Mr Gray to wait, Parker. I will come in in a few moments.'

Then he looked at Lord Henry. 'Dorian Gray is my dearest friend,' he said. 'He is a beautiful person. Don't spoil him. Don't try and influence him. Your influence would be bad. Don't take away from me the one person who makes me a true artist.'

'What silly things you say!' said Lord Henry. Smiling, he took Hallward by the arm and almost led him into the house.

Chapter 2   Jealous of his Own Portrait

As they entered they saw Dorian Gray. He was sitting at the piano, with his back to them, and he was turning the pages of some music by Schumann. 'You must lend me these, Basil,' he cried. 'I want to learn them. They are perfectly charming.'

'Perhaps if you sit well for me today, Dorian.'

'Oh, I am bored with sitting, and I don't want a portrait of myself,' answered the boy, turning quickly. When he saw Lord

5

Henry, his face went red for a moment. 'I am sorry, Basil. I didn't know that you had anyone with you.'

'This is Lord Henry Wotton, Dorian. He's an old friend of mine. We went to Oxford together. I have just been telling him what a good sitter you were, and now you have spoiled everything.'

'You have not spoiled my pleasure in meeting you, Mr Gray,' said Lord Henry, stepping forward and offering his hand. 'My aunt has often spoken to me about you.'

'I am afraid Lady Agatha is annoyed with me at the moment. I promised to go to a club in Whitechapel with her last Tuesday, and I forgot all about it. I don't know what she will say to me.'

Lord Henry looked at him. Yes, he was certainly wonderfully handsome, with his curved red lips, honest blue eyes and gold hair. 'Oh, don't worry about my aunt. You are one of her favourite people. And you are too charming to waste time working for poor people.'

Lord Henry sat down on the sofa and opened his cigarette box. The painter was busy mixing colours and getting his brushes ready. Suddenly, he looked at Lord Henry and said, 'Harry, I want to finish this picture today. Would you think it very rude of me if I asked you to go away?'

Lord Henry smiled, and looked at Dorian Gray. 'Shall I go, Mr Gray?' he asked.

'Oh, please don't, Lord Henry. I see that Basil is in one of his difficult moods, and I hate it when he is difficult. And I want you to tell me why I should not help the poor people.'

'That would be very boring, Mr Gray. But I certainly will not run away if you do not want me to. Is that all right, Basil? You have often told me that you like your sitters to have someone to talk to.'

Hallward bit his lip. 'If that is what Dorian wants. Dorian always gets what he wants.'

Lord Henry picked up his hat and gloves. 'No, I am afraid I must go. Goodbye, Mr Gray. Come and see me one afternoon in Curzon Street. I am nearly always at home at five o'clock.'

'Basil,' cried Dorian Gray, 'if Lord Henry Wotton goes, I will go too. You never open your lips while you are painting, and it is horribly boring just standing here. Ask him to stay.'

'All right, please stay, Harry. For Dorian and for me,' said Hallward, staring at his picture. 'It is true that I never talk when I am working, and never listen either. It must be very boring for my sitters. Sit down again, Harry. And Dorian don't move about too much, or listen to what Lord Henry says. He has a very bad influence over all his friends.'

Dorian Gray stood while Hallward finished his portrait. He liked what he had seen of Lord Henry. He was so different to Basil! And he had such a beautiful voice. After a few moments he said to him, 'Have you really a very bad influence, Lord Henry? As bad as Basil says?'

'Influence is always bad.'

'Why?'

'Because to influence someone is to give them your soul. Each person must have his own personality.'

'Turn your head a little more to the right, Dorian,' said the painter. He was not listening to the conversation and only knew that there was a new look on the boy's face.

'And yet,' continued Lord Henry, in his low musical voice, 'I believe that if one man lived his life fully and completely he could change the world. He would be a work of art greater than anything we have ever imagined. But the bravest man among us is afraid of himself. You, Mr Gray, are very young but you have had passions that have made you afraid, dreams –'

'Stop!' cried Dorian Gray, 'I don't understand what you are saying. I need to think.'

For nearly ten minutes he stood there with his lips open and his eyes strangely bright. The words that Basil's friend had spoken had

Lord Henry watched him. He knew the exact moment when to
say nothing.

touched his soul. Yes, there had been things in his boyhood that he had not understood. He understood them now.

With his smile, Lord Henry watched him. He knew the exact moment when to say nothing. He was surprised at the sudden effect of his words on the boy. How fascinating the boy was!

Hallward continued painting and did not notice that the others were silent.

'Basil, I am tired,' cried Dorian Gray, suddenly. 'I must go and sit in the garden. There is no air in here.'

'My dear boy, I am sorry. When I am painting, my work is all I can think about. But you never sat better. I don't know what Harry has been saying to you, but there is a wonderful bright look in your eyes. I suppose he has been flattering you. You shouldn't believe a word he says.'

'He has certainly not been flattering me. Perhaps that is why I don't believe anything he has told me.'

'You know you believe it all,' said Lord Henry, looking at him with his dreamy eyes. 'I will go out to the garden with you. It's horribly hot in this room.'

'Don't keep Dorian too long,' said the painter. 'This is going to be my best painting.'

Lord Henry went out to the garden, and found Dorian Gray holding a flower to his face. He came close to him, and put his hand on his shoulder.

Dorian Gray frowned and turned away. He liked the tall young man who was standing by him. His dark, romantic face interested him. There was something in his low, musical voice that was fascinating. But he felt a little afraid. Why was this stranger having a strong influence on him like this? He had known Basil Hallward for months, but the friendship between them had not changed him. Suddenly someone had come into his life and turned it upside down. Someone who seemed to have the key to the mystery of life itself.

And yet, what was there to be afraid of? He was not a schoolboy or a girl. It was silly to be afraid.

'Let us go and sit out of the sun. I don't want you to be burnt by the sun.'

'What does that matter?' cried Dorian Gray, laughing as he sat down on the seat at the end of the garden.

'It should matter very much to you, Mr Gray.'

'Why?'

'Because you are young, and to be young is the best thing in the world.'

'I don't feel that, Lord Henry.'

'No, you don't feel it now. Some day when you are old and ugly you will feel it terribly. Now, wherever you go, you charm the world. Will it always be so? . . . You have a wonderfully beautiful face, Mr Gray.'

'I don't think –'

'Don't frown. It is true. The gods have been good to you. But what the gods give they quickly take away. You have only a few years in which to really live, perfectly and fully. Live your life now, while you are still young!'

Suddenly the painter appeared at the door and waved at them to come in. They turned to each other and smiled.

'I am waiting,' he cried. 'Please come in. The light is perfect.'

They got up and walked towards the house together.

'You are glad you have met me, Mr Gray,' said Lord Henry, looking at him.

'Yes, I am glad now. I wonder whether I will always be glad.'

'Always! That is a terrible word. Women are so fond of using it.'

Twenty minutes later Hallward stopped painting. He stood back and looked at the portrait for a few moments. Then he bent down and signed his name in red paint on the bottom left-hand corner.

'It is finished,' he cried.

Lord Henry came over and examined the picture. It was certainly a wonderful work of art.

'My dear man,' he said. 'It is the best portrait of our time. Mr Gray, come over and look at yourself.'

Dorian walked across to look at the painting. When he saw it his cheeks went red with pleasure. He felt that he recognized his own beauty for the first time. But then he remembered what Lord Henry had said. His beauty would only be there for a few years. One day he would be old and ugly.

'Don't you like it?' cried Hallward, not understanding why the boy was silent.

'Of course he likes it,' said Lord Henry. 'It is one of the greatest paintings in modern art. I will pay anything you ask for it. I must have it.'

'It is not mine to sell, Harry.'

'Whose is it?'

'Dorian's, of course,' answered the painter.

'He is very lucky.'

'How sad it is!' said Dorian Gray, who was still staring at his own portrait. 'I will grow old and horrible. But this painting will always stay young. It will never be older than this day in June . . . if only it were the other way!'

'What do you mean?' asked Hallward.

'If I could stay young and the picture grow old! For that – for that – I would give everything! Yes, there is nothing in the whole world I would not give! I would give my soul for that!'

'I don't think you would like that, Basil,' cried Lord Henry, laughing.

'I certainly would not, Harry,' said Hallward.

Dorian Gray turned and looked at him. 'You like your art better than your friends.'

The painter stared in surprise. Why was Dorian speaking like that? What had happened? His face was red, and he seemed quite angry.

'You will always like this painting. But how long will you like me? Until I start getting old. Lord Henry Wotton is perfectly right. When I lose my beauty, I will lose everything. I shall kill myself before I get old.'

Hallward turned white, and caught his hand. 'Dorian! Dorian!' he cried. 'Don't talk like that. I have never had a friend like you, and I will never have another. How can you be jealous of a painting? You are more beautiful than any work of art.'

'I am jealous of everything whose beauty does not die. I am jealous of the portrait you have painted of me. Why should it keep what I must lose?' Hot tears came into his eyes as he threw himself on the sofa.

'You did this, Harry,' said the painter, angrily.

Lord Henry shook his head. 'It is the real Dorian Gray – that is all.'

'Harry, I can't argue with two of my best friends at once. Between you both you have made me hate the best piece of work I have ever done. I will destroy it.'

Dorian Gray watched as Hallward walked over to the painting-table and picked up a knife. The boy jumped from the sofa, tore the knife from Hallward's hand and threw it across the room. 'Don't, Basil!' he cried. 'Don't murder it!'

'I am glad that you like my work at last, Dorian,' said the painter coldly. 'I never thought you would.'

'Like it? I am in love with it, Basil. It is part of myself. I feel that.'

'What silly people you are, both of you!' said Lord Henry. 'Let's forget about the painting for one night and go to the theatre.'

'I would like to come to the theatre with you, Lord Henry.'

'And you will come too, won't you Basil?'

'I can't,' said Hallward. 'I have too much work to do.'

'Well, you and I will go together, Mr Gray.'

'Don't, Basil!' he cried. 'Don't murder it!'

The painter bit his lip and walked over to the picture.

'I will stay with the real Dorian,' he said sadly.

Chapter 3   Dorian in Love

One afternoon, a month later, Dorian Gray was sitting in the little library of Lord Henry's house in Mayfair. Lord Henry had not yet come in. He was always late. Dorian Gray was bored and once or twice he thought of going away.

At last he heard a step outside and the door opened. 'How late you are, Harry!' he said.

'I'm afraid it is not Harry, Mr Gray. It is only his wife.'

He looked around quickly and got to his feet. 'I am sorry. I thought –'

'I know you quite well by your photographs. I think my husband has got seventeen of them.'

'Seventeen, Lady Henry?'

'Well, eighteen, then. And I saw you with him the other night at the theatre. But here is Harry!'

Lord Henry smiled at them both. 'So sorry I am late, Dorian.'

'I am afraid I must go,' said Lady Harry. 'Goodbye, Mr Gray. Goodbye, Harry. You are eating out, I suppose? I am too. Perhaps I will see you later.'

'Perhaps, my dear,' said Lord Harry, shutting the door behind her. Then he lit a cigarette and threw himself down on the sofa.

'Never marry a woman with fair hair, Dorian,' he said.

'Why, Harry?'

'Because they are romantic.'

'But I like romantic people.'

'Never marry at all, Dorian.'

'I don't think I will marry, Harry. I am too much in love.'

'Who are you in love with?' asked Lord Henry, after a pause.

14

'I will stay with the real Dorian,' he said sadly.

'With an actress,' said Dorian Gray.

'How ordinary.'

'You would not say that if you saw her, Harry.'

'Who is she?'

'Her name is Sibyl Vane.'

'I've never heard of her.'

'No one has. People will some day, though. She is an artist.'

'My dear boy, no woman is an artist. Women never have anything to say but they say it charmingly. How long have you known her?'

'About three weeks.'

'And where did you meet her?'

'I will tell you, Harry, but you must not laugh. After all, it was you who gave me a passion to know everything about life. For days after I met you I searched the streets for beauty. I walked around the East End until I found a dirty little theatre. I see you are laughing. It is horrible of you!'

'I am not laughing, Dorian. Go on with your story.'

'The play was *Romeo and Juliet*. At first I was annoyed at the thought of seeing Shakespeare in such a terrible place. And when a fat old gentleman came out as Romeo I nearly walked out. But then I saw Juliet! Harry, she was the loveliest thing I had ever seen in my life.'

'When did you meet her?'

'I went back the next night and the night after that. On the third evening I waited for her outside the theatre.'

'What was she like?'

'Sibyl? Oh, she was shy and gentle. She is only seventeen and there is something of a child in her. She said to me, "You look like a prince. I must call you Prince Charming".'

'Miss Sibyl knows how to flatter you.'

'You don't understand her, Harry. She thinks that I am like a person in Shakespeare. She knows nothing of life. Sibyl is the only thing I care about.'

'That is the reason, I suppose, that you never have dinner with me now. I thought it might be something romantic.'

'My dear Harry, we eat together every day,' said Dorian.

'You always come very late.'

'Well, I have to see Sibyl play,' he cried.

'Can you have dinner with me tonight, Dorian?'

He shook his head. 'Tonight she is Ophelia,' he answered, 'and tomorrow night she will be Juliet.'

'When is she Sibyl Vane?'

'Never.'

'That's good.'

'How horrible you are! But when you see her you will think differently. I want you and Basil to come and watch her tomorrow night. You are certain to recognize that she is wonderful.'

'All right. Tomorrow evening. Will you see Basil before then? Or shall I write to him?'

'Dear Basil! I haven't seen him for a week. It is rather horrible of me as he sent me my portrait a few days ago. I love looking at it. Perhaps you should write to him. I don't want to see him alone. He says things that annoy me. He gives me good advice.'

Lord Henry smiled. 'People are very fond of giving away advice they need themselves.'

'Oh, Basil is a good man, but I don't think he really understands about art and beauty. Since I have known you, Harry, I have discovered that.'

'Basil, my dear boy, puts everything that is charming in him into his work.'

'I must go now, Harry. My Juliet is waiting for me. Don't forget about tomorrow. Goodbye.'

'I want you and Basil to come and watch Sibyl tomorrow night.
You are certain to recognize that she is wonderful.'

As Dorian left the room, Lord Henry began to think about what he had just learned. Certainly few people had ever interested him so much as Dorian Gray. Yet the mad worship of this actress did not make him annoyed or jealous. He was pleased by it. It made the boy more interesting to study.

Later that night, when he arrived home from dinner, Lord Henry saw a telegram on the table near the door. He opened it and read that Dorian Gray was going to marry Sibyl Vane.

Chapter 4   The Worship of Sybil Vane

'I suppose you have heard the news, Basil?' said Lord Henry the following evening. They were in the dining-room of the Bristol Hotel.

'No, Harry,' answered the artist, giving his hat and coat to the waiter. 'What is it?'

'Dorian Gray is going to be married,' said Lord Henry, watching him as he spoke.

Hallward frowned. 'Dorian going to be married!' he cried. 'Impossible!'

'It is perfectly true.'

'To whom?'

'To some little actress.'

'But it would be absurd for him to marry someone like that.'

'If you want to make him marry this girl tell him that, Basil. He is sure to do it, then. Whenever a man does a completely stupid thing, it is always for a good reason.'

'I hope this girl is good, Harry.'

'Oh, she is better than good – she is beautiful,' said Lord Henry. 'Dorian says that she is beautiful and he is not often wrong about these things. Your portrait has helped him understand beauty in others. We are to see her tonight, if that boy doesn't forget.'

'But how can Dorian marry an actress, Harry? It is absurd,' cried the painter, walking up and down the room, biting his lip.

'Dorian Gray falls in love with a beautiful actress who plays Juliet. He asks her to marry him. Why not? I hope that Dorian Gray marries this girl and worships her for six months. Then he can suddenly become fascinated by another woman.'

'You don't mean a word of that, Harry! I know you don't really want Dorian Gray's life to be spoiled. You are much better than you pretend to be.'

Lord Henry laughed. 'The reason we all like to think so well of others is because we are afraid for ourselves. But here is Dorian himself. He will tell you more than I can.'

'My dear Harry, my dear Basil, you must both congratulate me!' said the boy, throwing off his coat and shaking each of his friends' hands. 'I have never been so happy. Of course it is sudden – all the best things are. And yet it seems to me to be the one thing I have been looking for all my life.'

'I hope you will always be very happy, Dorian,' said Hallward, 'but why did you not tell me? You told Harry.'

'There really is not much to tell,' cried Dorian. 'Last night I went to see her again. After, when we were sitting together, there came into her eyes a wonderful look. It was something I had never seen there before. We kissed each other. I can't describe to you what I felt at that moment.'

'Have you seen her today?' asked Lord Henry.

Dorian Gray shook his head. 'I have left her in Shakespeare's forest. I will find her in his garden.'

'At what exact point did you use the word "marry", Dorian? And how did she answer? Perhaps you forgot all about it.'

'My dear Harry, it was not a business meeting. I told her I loved her. The whole world is nothing to me compared to her.'

'But my dear Dorian –'

Hallward put his hand on Lord Henry's arm. 'Don't Harry. You have annoyed Dorian. He is not like other men. He would never harm anyone.'

Lord Henry looked across the table. 'Dorian is never annoyed with me,' he answered.

Dorian Gray laughed. 'When I am with Sibyl Vane I don't believe in anything you have taught me. I forget all your fascinating, terrible ideas.'

'And those are . . .?' asked Lord Henry, helping himself to some salad.

'Oh, your ideas about life, your ideas about love, your ideas about pleasure. All your ideas, Harry.'

'Pleasure is the only thing worth having ideas about,' he answered, in his slow, musical voice. 'When we are happy we are always good, but when we are good we are not always happy.'

'I know what pleasure is,' cried Dorian Gray. 'It is to worship someone.'

'That is certainly better than when someone worships you.'

'Harry, you are terrible! I don't know why I like you so much. Let us go down to the theatre. When you see Sibyl you will change your ideas.'

They got up and put on their coats. The painter was silent and thoughtful. He felt very sad. Dorian Gray would never again be to him all that he had been in the past. Life had come between them.

When he arrived at the theatre it seemed to Hallward that he had grown years older.

Chapter 5   Dorian Leaves Sybil

The theatre was crowded that night. It was terribly hot and there were young people shouting to each other from across seats. Women were laughing loudly and their voices sounded horrible. People were eating oranges and drinking from bottles.

'What a place to find the perfect girl in!' said Lord Henry.

'Yes!' answered Dorian Gray. 'It was here I found her. When you see her as Juliet you will forget everything. These ugly people become quite different when she appears.'

'I understand what you mean, Dorian,' said the painter, 'and I believe in this girl. Anyone you love must be wonderful.'

'Thanks, Basil,' answered Dorian Gray. 'I knew that you would understand me. In a few minutes you will see the girl who I am going to give my life to. The girl who I have given everything that is good in me.'

Then Sibyl appeared. The crowd shouted and called her name. Yes, she was certainly lovely to look at, Lord Henry thought. Basil Hallward jumped to his feet excitedly. Dorian Gray sat staring at her like he was in a dream.

'Charming! Charming!' cried Lord Henry.

A quarter of an hour later, Lord Henry whispered to Hallward. 'She's one of the loveliest girls I have ever seen. But she is a terrible actress.'

Dorian Gray's face turned white as he watched her speak. She was so different tonight! Now she was not Juliet but a very bad actress who did not understand Shakespeare's words.

Even the crowd became bored and began to talk loudly. The only person who did not seem to notice was the actress herself.

Lord Henry got up from his chair and put on his coat. 'She is beautiful, Dorian,' he said, 'but she can't act. Let's go.'

Then Sibyl appeared. Yes, she was certainly lovely to look at,
Lord Henry thought.

'I am going to stay until the end,' answered the boy in a cold voice. 'I am awfully sorry that I have made you waste an evening, Harry. I apologize to you both.'

'My dear Dorian, perhaps Miss Vane is ill,' said Hallward. 'We will come some other night.'

'Come to the club with Basil and myself. We will smoke cigarettes and drink to the beauty of Sibyl Vane. She is beautiful. What more do you want?'

'Go away, Harry,' cried the boy. 'I want to be alone. Can't you see my heart is breaking?' Hot tears came to his eyes as Lord Henry and Hallward left the theatre.

When it was over, Dorian Gray rushed to see Sibyl Vane. The girl was standing there alone, with a look of extraordinary happiness on her face.

'How badly I acted tonight, Dorian!' she cried.

'Horribly!' he answered, staring at her. 'It was terrible. Are you ill? Why did you make me suffer like that?'

The girl smiled. 'Dorian, don't you understand?'

'Understand what?' he asked, angrily.

'Why I was so bad tonight. Why I will always be bad. Why I will never act well again.'

'You are ill, I suppose. When you are ill, you shouldn't act. My friends were bored. I was bored.'

'Dorian, Dorian,' she cried, 'before I knew you, acting was the one important thing in my life. It was only in the theatre that I lived. I thought that it was all true. Tonight, for the first time in my life I saw that I was playing at love. Our love for each other is the only true love. Take me away with you, Dorian! I don't want to be an actress any more.'

He threw himself down on the sofa, and turned away his face. 'You have killed my love,' he said quietly. Then he jumped up and went to the door. 'My God! How mad I was to love you! What a fool I have been! You are nothing to me now. I will

'Take me away with you, Dorian! I don't want to be an actress any more.'

never see you again. I will never think of you. I will never speak to you again.'

The girl went white. 'You are not serious, Dorian? You are acting?' she whispered, putting her hand on his arm.

He pushed her back. 'Don't touch me!' he cried. Then he turned and left the room.

After walking the streets of London all night, he arrived home just after sunrise. As he passed through the library, he saw the portrait that Basil Hallward had painted of him. He stared at it in surprise and walked on into his bedroom. He took his coat off and stood next to his bed. A few moments later he returned to the picture and looked at it closely. In the poor light the face seemed to have changed a little. Now the mouth looked cruel. It was certainly strange.

He walked to the window and opened the curtains. The light changed the room, but the face stayed the same. In fact, the sunlight made the mouth look even crueller.

Going back to his bedroom, he found a small mirror that had been a present from Lord Henry. He looked at his real face and saw no sign of cruelty. What did it mean?

He threw himself into a chair, and began to think. Suddenly he remembered what he had said in Basil Hallward's house the day the picture had been finished. Yes, he remembered it perfectly. He had asked that the painting grow old so that he himself could remain young. But such things were impossible. It was terrible even to think about them. And, yet, there was the picture in front of him. There was the cruelty in the mouth.

Cruelty! Had he been cruel? No, why think about Sibyl Vane? She was nothing to him now.

But the picture? What was he to say of that? It held the secret of his life, and told his story. It had taught him to love his own beauty.

Would it teach him to hate his own soul? Would he ever look at it again?

He would save himself! He would not see Lord Henry again. He would go back to Sibyl Vane, marry her and try to love her again. She had suffered more than he had. Poor child! He had been selfish and cruel to her. They would be happy together. His life with her would be beautiful and pure.

He got up from his chair, and covered the portrait. 'How horrible!' he said to himself, and he walked across to the window and opened it. When he stepped out on to the grass he took a deep breath. He thought only of Sibyl. The birds that were singing in the garden seemed to be telling the flowers about her.

Chapter 6   Love Becomes Tragedy

It was nearly one o'clock the next afternoon when he woke up. His servant brought him a cup of tea and some letters. One of them was from Lord Henry, and had been brought by hand that morning. He put it to one side.

He went into the library for breakfast feeling perfectly happy. Then he saw the open window and the covered portrait. Was it all true? Or had it just been a dream? But he remembered that cruel mouth so clearly.

Dorian Gray sent his servant away and locked all the doors. Then he pulled the cover off the painting, and saw himself face to face. It was true. The portrait had changed.

For hours he did not know what to do or think. Finally, he went over to the table and wrote a passionate letter to the girl he had loved. He asked her to forgive him for the terrible things he had said to her.

Suddenly he heard a knock on the door, and he heard Lord Henry's voice outside. 'My dear boy, I must see you.'

Suddenly he heard a knock on the door, and he heard Lord Henry's voice outside. 'My dear boy, I must see you. Let me in at once.'

He made no answer, but remained quite still. The knocking continued and grew louder. Yes, it was better to let Lord Henry in. He would explain to him the new life he was going to lead. He jumped up, covered the picture and opened the door.

'I am sorry about it all, Dorian,' said Lord Henry, as he entered. 'But you must not think too much about it.'

'Do you mean about Sibyl Vane?' asked the boy.

'Yes, of course,' answered Lord Henry, sitting down and slowly pulling off his yellow gloves. 'It is terrible, but you are not to blame. Tell me, did you go behind and see her after it was over?'

'Yes.'

'I felt sure that you had. Did you have an argument?'

'I was cruel, Harry – terribly cruel. But it is all right now. I am not sorry for anything that has happened. It has taught me to know myself better.'

'Oh, Dorian, I am so glad that you see it that way.'

'I want to be good, Harry. I don't want my soul to be ugly. I am going to marry Sibyl Vane.'

'Marry Sibyl Vane!' cried Lord Henry, standing up, and staring at him in surprise. 'But, my dear Dorian –'

'Yes, Harry, I know what you are going to say. Something horrible about getting married. Don't say it! Sibyl will be my wife!'

'Your wife! Dorian! . . . Didn't you get my letter? I wrote to you this morning.'

'Your letter? Oh, yes, I remember. I have not read it yet, Harry.'

'You know nothing yet then?'

'What do you mean?'

Lord Henry walked across the room and sat down next to Dorian Gray. Taking both his hands in his own, he held them. 'Dorian,' he said, 'my letter was to tell you that Sibyl Vane is dead.'

A cry of pain came from the boy's lips and he jumped to his feet. 'Dead! Sibyl dead! It is not true! It is a horrible lie!'

'It is true, Dorian,' said Lord Henry. 'It is in all the morning newspapers. The police will be asking questions, and you must keep your name out of any scandal. Things like that make a man fashionable in Paris. But in London they are a disaster for any gentleman. I suppose they don't know your name at the theatre? If they don't, it is all right. Did anyone see you going round to her room?'

Dorian did not answer for a few moments. Finally he said in a strange voice, 'Harry, did you say that the police are asking questions? What did you mean by that? Did Sibyl –? Oh, Harry this is terrible!'

'I am sure that it was not an accident, though it must be described that way officially. She swallowed something horrible they use at theatres.'

'Harry, Harry, it is terrible!' cried the boy.

'Yes, it is very sad, of course, but it is nothing to do with you. Come with me to dinner, and after we will go to the theatre.'

'So I have murdered Sibyl Vane,' said Dorian Gray, half to himself. 'Yet the roses are not less lovely. The birds still sing happily in my garden. And tonight I will have dinner with you and go to the theatre. How extraordinary life is! My first passionate love letter was to a dead girl. Yet why is it that I cannot feel this tragedy as much as I want to? I don't think I am heartless. Do you?'

'You have done too many foolish things in the last fortnight to be heartless, Dorian,' answered Lord Henry, with his sweet, sad smile.

The boy frowned. 'I don't like that explanation, Harry,' he said, 'but I am glad you don't think I am heartless.'

'A woman has killed herself for the love of you,' said Lord Henry. 'That is very beautiful.'

They were silent. The evening darkened in the room. After some time Dorian Gray looked up. 'How well you know me! But we

A cry of pain came from the boy's lips and he jumped to his feet.
'Dead! Sibyl dead! It is not true! It is a horrible lie!'

will not talk again of what has happened. It has been something wonderful. That is all. Now, I have to dress, Harry. I feel too tired to eat anything, but I will join you later at the theatre.'

As Lord Henry closed the door behind him Dorian rushed to the portrait and tore off the cover. No, there was no further change in the picture. It had received the news of Sibyl Vane's death before he had known of it himself. Tears came to his eyes as he remembered her. He brushed them away and looked again at the picture.

He felt the time had come to choose. Or had he already chosen? Yes, life had decided that for him. The portrait was going to carry his shame: that was all.

An hour later he was at the theatre, and Lord Henry was sitting beside him.

Chapter 7   'What Is Past Is Past'

As he was eating breakfast the next morning, Basil Hallward was shown into the room.

'I am so glad I have found you, Dorian,' he said. 'I called last night, and they told me that you were at the theatre. Of course I knew that was impossible. I had a terrible evening worrying whether one tragedy would be followed by another. I can't tell you how heart-broken I am about the whole thing. Did you go and see the girl's mother? What did she say about it all?'

'My dear Basil, I don't know,' said Dorian Gray. He looked very bored. 'I was at the theatre.'

'You went to the theatre?' said Hallward, speaking very slowly. 'You went to the theatre where Sibyl Vane was lying dead?'

'Stop, Basil! I won't hear it!' cried Dorian, jumping to his feet. 'You must not speak of such things. What is done is done. What is past is past.'

'You call yesterday the past? Dorian, this is horrible! Something has changed you completely. You look exactly the same as the wonderful boy in my picture, but now there is no heart in you. It is all Harry's influence. I see that.'

The boy went to the window and looked out at the garden for a few moments.

'Harry has taught me many things, Basil,' he said at last. 'You have only taught me to love my own beauty.'

'I am truly sorry for that, Dorian.'

'I don't know what you mean, Basil,' he said, turning round. 'I don't know what you want. What do you want?'

'I want the Dorian Gray I used to paint,' said the artist sadly.

'Basil,' said the boy, going over to him and putting his hand on his shoulder, 'you have come too late. Yesterday when I heard that Sibyl Vane had killed herself –'

'Killed herself! My God! Is there no doubt about that?' cried Hallward.

'My dear Basil! Of course she killed herself.'

The older man put his face in his hands. 'How terrible,' he said in a quiet voice.

'No,' said Dorian Gray, 'there is nothing terrible about it. It is one of the great romantic tragedies of our time. I know you are surprised at me talking to you like this. You have not realized how I have changed. I was a boy when you knew me. I am a man now. I have new passions, new thoughts, new ideas –'

'But Dorian –'

'I am different, but you must not like me less. Of course I am very fond of Harry. But I know that you are better than he is. You are not stronger – you are too afraid of life – but you are better. And how happy we used to be together! Don't leave me, Basil, and don't argue with me. I am what I am.'

The painter felt strangely sad. Dorian Gray was extraordinarily important to him. The boy had changed his art. Perhaps his cruel talk about Sibyl Vane was just a mood that would pass away. There was so much in him that was good.

'Well, Dorian,' he said with a sad smile, 'I won't speak to you again about this horrible thing. I only hope that your name is kept out of any scandal. Have the police asked to see you?'

Dorian shook his head. 'They don't even know my name,' he answered.

'She didn't know your name?'

'Only my first name, and I am sure that she did not tell it to anyone. She told her family that I was Prince Charming. It was pretty of her. You must do me a drawing of Sibyl, Basil. I would like to have something more of her than the memory of a few kisses.'

'I will try and do something, Dorian. But you must come and sit for me again. I can't work so well without you.'

'I can never sit for you again, Basil. It is impossible!' he cried.

'My dear boy, what is this foolishness!' Hallward cried. 'Did you not like what I did for you? Where is it? Why have you covered it? Let me look at it. It is the best thing I have ever done. It is very bad of your servant to hide my work like that. I felt the room looked different as I came in.'

'It was not my servant who covered it, Basil. I did it myself. The light was too strong on the portrait.'

'Too strong! No, the light is perfect in here. Let me see it.' And Hallward walked towards the corner of the room.

A terrible cry came from Dorian Gray's lips, and he rushed between the painter and the covered portrait. 'Basil, you must not look at it! I don't want you to.'

'Not look at my own work! Are you serious? Why shouldn't I look at it?' cried Hallward, laughing.

'If you try and look at it, Basil, I promise I will never speak to you again. I am very serious.'

Hallward looked at Dorian Gray in surprise. He had never seem him like this before. The boy's face was white and angry.

*A terrible cry came from Dorian Gray's lips, and he rushed between
the painter and the covered portrait.*

'Dorian!'

'Don't speak!'

'But what is the matter? Of course I won't look at it if you don't want me to,' he said coldly, walking over to the window. 'But it seems rather absurd that I cannot see my own work when I am going to exhibit it in Paris in the autumn.'

'To exhibit it? You want to exhibit it?' cried Dorian Gray. A terrible fear was building inside him. Was the world going to see his secret? Were people going to stare at the mystery of his life? That was impossible.

'Yes, George Petit is going to exhibit all my best pictures in October. Don't worry, it is only for one month.'

Dorian Gray passed his hand across his face. It felt hot and wet. He felt that he was about to face horrible danger. 'You told me a month ago that you would never exhibit it,' he cried. 'Why have you changed your mind?' He stopped suddenly and a cruel look came into his eyes. He had remembered something Lord Henry had said to him, *'Ask Basil why he won't exhibit your picture. He told me once and it is a very strange story.'* Yes, perhaps Basil, too, had his secret. He would ask him and try.

'Basil,' he said, coming over quite close, and looking him straight in the face. 'We all have secrets. What was your reason for not wanting to exhibit my picture?'

'Dorian, if I told you, you might like me less than you do now. And you would certainly laugh at me. If you don't want me ever to look at your picture again, I won't. I have always you to look at. Your friendship is more important to me than exhibiting a painting.'

'No, Basil, you must tell me,' said Dorian Gray. His feeling of fear had passed away. Now he just wanted to find out Basil Hallward's mystery.

'Dorian,' said the painter, who did not look happy. 'Have you ever noticed something in the picture, something strange?'

'Basil!' cried the boy, staring at him with wild eyes.

'I see you did. Dorian, from the moment I met you, your personality had the most extraordinary influence over me. I worshipped you. I was jealous of everyone you spoke to. I wanted to have you all to myself. I was only happy when I was with you. When you were away from me you were still there in my art.'

'Basil —'

'No, don't speak. I must tell you now what I did not tell you then. That I decided to paint a wonderful portrait of you. I put all my feelings for you into that picture. I felt, Dorian, that I had told too much. I had put too much of myself into it. So I decided never to exhibit the portrait. I told Harry and he laughed. When the picture was finished, and I sat alone with it, I felt that I was right . . . Later, I thought that perhaps I was being foolish and when this Paris offer came . . . but I see now that the picture cannot be shown.'

Dorian Gray breathed deeply. The colour came back to his cheeks and a smile crossed his lips. The danger was over and he was safe for a while. What a sad story Basil had told. Would he ever be so influenced by the personality of a friend? Lord Henry had the charm of being very dangerous. But that was all.

'It is extraordinary to me, Dorian,' said Hallward, 'that you saw this in the portrait.'

'I saw something in it,' he answered, 'something that seemed to me very strange.'

'Well, you don't mind me looking at the thing now?'

Dorian shook his head. 'You must not ask me that, Basil. I cannot let you stand in front of that picture.'

'You will one day, won't you?'

'Never.'

'Well, perhaps you are right. And now goodbye, Dorian. You have been the one person in my life who has really influenced my art. But you don't know what it cost me to tell you all that I have told you.'

'My dear Basil,' said Dorian, 'what have you told me? Only that you worshipped me too much. That is not even flattery.'

'It was not meant as flattery. And now that I have told you, something seems to have gone out of me. Perhaps you should never put what you worship into words.'

'You mustn't talk about worship. It is foolish. You and I are friends, Basil, and we will always be friends.'

'You have got Harry,' said the painter, sadly.

'Oh, Harry!' laughed the young man. 'Harry spends his life saying and doing extraordinary things. He lives the sort of life I want to live. But I don't think I would go to Harry if I was in trouble. I would prefer to go to you, Basil.'

'You will sit for me again?'

'Impossible! There is something terrible about a portrait. It has a life of its own. I will come and have tea with you instead.'

'Well, goodbye then. I am sorry that you won't let me look at the picture again. But I understand what you feel about it.'

As he left the room, Dorian Gray smiled to himself. Poor Basil! How little he knew of the true reason. And now he understood more the painter's wild and jealous feelings, and he felt sorry. There was something tragic in a friendship so corrupted by passion.

He rang the bell to call his servant. He had to hide the portrait immediately. It had been mad of him to leave it in a place where it could be discovered by his friends.

Chapter 8   The Portrait Is Hidden

When the servant entered, Dorian Gray asked him to send Mrs Leaf to him in the library. Mrs Leaf had been with his family for many years. He asked her for the key to the old schoolroom.

As he left the room, Dorian Gray smiled to himself. Poor Basil! How little he knew of the true reason.

'The old schoolroom, Mr Dorian?' she cried. 'But it is full of dust! I must clean it first.'

'I don't want it cleaned, Mrs Leaf. I only want the key.'

'Well, sir, you'll be covered with dust if you go into it. It hasn't been open for nearly five years, not since your grandfather died.'

He frowned at this reminder of his grandfather. He had bad memories of all his family. 'That does not matter,' he answered. 'I just want to see the place – that is all. Give me the key.'

'Here is the key, sir,' said the old lady. 'But you are not going to live up there, are you, sir?'

'No, no,' he cried. 'Thank you, Mrs Leaf. You can go.'

An hour later two men arrived to move the portrait.

'It's very heavy, sir,' said one of the men, as they climbed the stairs.

'I am afraid it is rather heavy,' said Dorian, as he opened the door of the old schoolroom where he was going to hide the secret of his corrupted soul.

He had not entered the room since he was a child. It was a large room built by his grandfather to keep him at a distance. Every moment of his lonely childhood came back to him as he looked round.

It was a room full of terrible memories, but it was safe. He had the key, and no other person could enter it. The face in the portrait could grow old and ugly. What did it matter? No one could see it. He himself would not see it. He did not have to watch the terrible corruption of his soul. He would stay young – that was enough.

When the men had gone, Dorian locked the door, and put the key in his pocket. He felt safe now. No one would ever look at that horrible thing. Only he would ever see his shame.

'It's very heavy, sir,' said one of the men, as they climbed the stairs.

He went back to the library and found a note from Lord Henry. In it was a report from the newspaper about Sibyl Vane. Her death was officially described as an accident.

He frowned, and tore the paper in two. Then he walked across the room and threw the pieces away. How ugly it all was! And how horribly real ugliness made things!

Perhaps the servant had read the report, and had begun to suspect something. And, yet, what did it matter? What had Dorian Gray to do with Sibyl Vane's death? There was nothing to be afraid of. Dorian Gray had not killed her.

Chapter 9   'I Will Show You my Soul'

Many years passed. Yet the wonderful beauty that had so fascinated Basil Hallward, stayed with Dorian Gray. Even those who had heard terrible rumours against him, could not believe them when they met him. He always had the look of someone who had kept himself pure.

Many people suspected that there was something very wrong with Dorian's life, but only he knew about the portrait. Some nights he would secretly enter the locked room. Holding a mirror in his hand, he would stand in front of the picture Basil Hallward had painted. He would look first at the horrible, old face in the picture, and then at the handsome young face that laughed back at him from the mirror. He fell more and more in love with his own beauty. And more and more interested in the corruption of his own soul.

Then something happened that changed everything.

It was on the ninth of November, the day before his thirty-eighth birthday. He was walking home from Lord Henry's and the night was cold and foggy. At the corner of Grovesnor Square and South Audley Street, a man passed him in the fog. He was walking very fast, and had the collar of his coat turned up. He had a bag in his hand. Dorian recognized him. It was Basil Hallward. A strange fear made Dorian walk off quickly in the direction of his own house.

But Hallward had seen him. Dorian heard him hurrying after him. In a few moments his hand was on his arm.

'Dorian! What an extraordinary piece of luck! I have been waiting for you in your library ever since nine o'clock. I am going to Paris on the midnight train, and I wanted to see you before I left. I thought it was you, or at least your coat, as I passed you. But I wasn't sure. Didn't you recognize me?'

'In this fog, my dear Basil? I can't even recognize Grosvenor Square. I believe my house is somewhere about here, but I don't feel at all certain about it. I am sorry you are going away, as I have not seen you for such a long time. But I suppose you will be back soon?'

'No, I am going to be out of England for six months. Here we are at your door. Let me come in for a moment. I have something to say to you.'

'That would be lovely. But won't you miss your train?' said Dorian Gray, as he went up the steps and opened the door with his key.

'I have plenty of time,' he answered. 'The train doesn't go until twelve-fifteen, and it is only just eleven. All I have with me is this bag, and I can easily get to Victoria Station in twenty minutes.'

Dorian looked at him and smiled. 'Come in or the fog will get into my house.'

Hallward followed Dorian into the library. There was a bright wood fire on one side of the room and two lamps on the other.

'Would you like a drink?' asked Dorian.

'No thanks, I won't have anything more,' said the painter, taking his hat and coat off. 'And now, my dear Dorian, I want to speak to

'I think you should know some of the terrible things that people are saying about you.'

you seriously. Don't frown like that. You make it so much more difficult for me.'

'What is it all about?' cried Dorian, throwing himself down on the sofa. 'I hope it is not about myself. I am tired of myself tonight. I would prefer to be somebody different.'

'It is about yourself,' answered Hallward, in his deep voice, 'and I must say it to you.'

Dorian breathed deeply and lit a cigarette. 'Is it really necessary, Basil?'

'I think you should know some of the terrible things that people are saying about you.'

'I don't want to know anything about them. I love scandals about other people, but scandals about myself don't interest me.'

'Every gentleman is interested in his good name, Dorian. You don't want people to talk of you as something terrible and corrupt. But I don't believe these rumours at all. At least I can't believe them when I see you. Corruption is a thing that writes itself across a man's face. It cannot be hidden.'

'My dear Basil —'

'And yet, I rarely see you now and you never come to my house. When I hear all the terrible things people are whispering about you, I don't know what to say. Why have so many of your friends killed themselves? Young men from good families like Adrian Singleton and that poor young soldier?'

'Stop, Basil. You are talking about things of which you know nothing,' said Dorian. 'I know how people talk in England. This is a country where people have two faces. They whisper rumours about people like myself, and then do much worse things when others are not looking.'

'Dorian,' cried Hallward, 'that is not the question. I know England is bad, but that's the reason I want you to be a good influence on your friends. Instead you have lost all belief in goodness and honesty. You have filled those poor young men with a madness for pleasure.'

Dorian smiled.

'How can you smile like that? I only want you to have a clean name. You have a wonderful influence. Let it be for good. Yet I wonder whether I know you? But I can't answer that question. I would need to see your soul.'

'To see my soul!' cried Dorian Gray. He jumped up from the sofa, turning almost white with fear.

'Yes,' answered Hallward. There was a deep sadness in his voice. 'To see your soul. But only God can do that.'

A bitter laugh came from the lips of the younger man. 'You will see it yourself, tonight!' he cried, picking up a lamp from the table. 'Come: it is your own work. Why shouldn't you look at it? You can tell the world all about it after, if you want. Nobody will believe you. If they do believe you, they will like me better for it. Come, I tell you. You have talked enough about corruption. Now you will see it face to face.'

There was madness in every word he said. He felt a terrible delight that someone was going to share his secret. The man who had painted the portrait was going to share his shame. The painter would suffer for the rest of his life with the memory of what he had done.

'Yes,' he continued, coming closer to him. 'I will show you my soul. You will see what you think only God can see.'

Hallward jumped back.

'You cannot say things like that, Dorian!' he cried. 'They are horrible and they don't mean anything.'

'You think so?' He laughed again.

'I know so. Dorian, you have to tell me –'

'Don't touch me. Finish what you have to say.'

The painter felt extraordinarily sad. He walked over to the fire and stood there.

'I am waiting, Basil,' said the young man, in a hard, clear voice.

He turned round. 'What I have to say is this,' he cried. 'You must give me some answer to the horrible things people are saying against you. Tell me that they are not true, Dorian! Can't you see what I am going through? My God! Don't tell me that you are bad and corrupt and shameful.'

Dorian Gray smiled. 'Come upstairs, Basil,' he said, quietly. 'I keep a diary of my life from day to day. I will show it to you if you come up with me.'

'I will come with you, Dorian, if you wish it. I see I have missed my train. It does not matter. I can go tomorrow. But don't ask me to read anything tonight. All I want is a simple answer to my question.'

'I will give it to you upstairs. I could not give it to you here. You will not have to read for long.'

Chapter 10   Basil Sees the Portrait

He passed out of the room and began climbing the stairs. Basil Hallward followed close behind. They walked softly, as people always do at night. The lamp made strange shadows on the wall and stairs.

When they reached the top, Dorian put the lamp down on the floor. He took the key out of his pocket and turned it in the lock.

'You really want to know, Basil?' he asked in a low voice.

'Yes.'

'I am delighted,' he answered, smiling. Then he added, 'You are the one man in the world I want to know everything about me. You have influenced my life more than you think.' Taking up the lamp, he opened the door and went in. Cold air passed between them. 'Shut the door behind you,' he whispered, as he placed the lamp on the table.

Hallward looked around the room in surprise. The room had clearly not been lived in for years. The whole place was covered with dust, and there were holes in the carpet. A mouse ran across the floor.

'So you think that it is only God who sees the soul, Basil. Take the cover off the portrait, and you will see mine.'

The voice that spoke was cold and cruel.

'You are mad, Dorian,' said Hallward, frowning.

'You won't take the cover off? Then I will do it myself,' said the young man, throwing the old purple curtain to the ground.

A cry of fear came from the painter's lips when he saw the face in the portrait. It was Dorian Gray's face he was looking at, and it still had some of that wonderful beauty. But now there were terrible signs of age and corruption. But who had done it? He held the lamp up to the picture. In the left hand corner was his name, painted in red.

What had happened? He had never done that. Still, it was his own picture. He knew it, and it made his blood turn to ice. His own picture! What did it mean? Why had it changed? He turned, and looked at Dorian Gray with the eyes of a sick man.

The young man was standing near the wall, watching him. He had taken the flower out of his coat, and was smelling it.

'What does this mean?' cried Hallward, at last. His own voice sounded high and strange.

'Years ago, when I was a boy,' said Dorian Gray, closing his hand on the flower, 'you met me and flattered me. You taught me to love my beauty. One day you introduced me to a friend of yours. He explained to me how wonderful it was to be young. You finished a portrait of me that showed me how wonderful it was to be beautiful. In a mad moment I made a wish –'

'I remember it! Oh, how well I remember it! No! The thing is

48

impossible. There must be something wrong with the paint. I tell you the thing is impossible.'

'Is anything really impossible?' said the young man, going over to the window.

'You told me you had destroyed it.'

'I was wrong. It has destroyed me.'

'I don't believe it is my picture. There was nothing bad in it, nothing shameful. You were perfect to me. This is a face from hell.'

'It is the face of my soul. Each of us has Heaven and Hell in him, Basil,' cried Dorian wildly.

Hallward turned again to the portrait, and stared at it. 'My God! Is this true?' he cried. 'Is this what you have done with your life? You must be even worse than people say!'

Hallward threw himself into the chair by the table and put his face in his hands. The lamp fell to the floor and went out.

'Good God, Dorian! What an awful lesson! What an awful lesson!' There was no answer, but he could hear the young man crying at the window. 'We must ask God for forgiveness. I worshipped you too much. I am punished for it. You worshipped yourself too much. We are both punished.'

Dorian Gray turned slowly around and looked at him. There were tears in his eyes. 'It is too late, Basil,' he said.

'But don't you see that hellish thing staring at us?'

Dorian Gray looked at the picture. Suddenly he felt that he hated Basil Hallward. He hated the man sitting at the table more than he hated anything in his life.

He looked wildly around. Something shone on top of the painted cupboard that faced him. It was a knife he had left there some days before. He moved slowly towards it, passing Hallward as he did so. He took the knife in his hand and turned around. Hallward moved in his chair. He rushed at him, and stuck the knife into his neck again and again.

Dorian threw the knife down on the table and stood back. He could hear nothing but the sound of blood falling on to the carpet.

He threw the knife down on the table and stood back. He could hear nothing but the sound of blood falling on to the carpet. He opened the door and went out on to the stairs. The house was completely quiet. No one was there.

How quickly it had all been done! Feeling strangely calm, he walked over to the window and opened it. The wind had blown the fog away and the sky was clear. He looked down and saw a policeman walking down the street. He was shining a lamp in all the houses.

Closing the window, he went back into the room. He did not look at the murdered man. He felt that the secret of the whole thing was not to think about it at all. The friend who had painted the terrible portrait had gone out of his life. That was enough.

He picked up the lamp and walked out of the room, locking the door behind him. As he walked down the stairs he thought that he heard what sounded like cries of pain. He stopped several times, and waited. No, everything was still.

When he reached the library, he saw the bag and coat in the corner. They must be hidden away somewhere. He unlocked a secret cupboard and threw them in. He could easily burn them later. Then he pulled out his watch. It was twenty minutes to two.

He sat down and began to think. Basil Hallward had left the house at eleven. No one had seen him come in again. The servants were in bed . . . Paris! Yes. It was to Paris that Basil had gone. And by the midnight train as he had planned. It would be months before anyone suspected anything. Months! He could destroy everything long before then.

Suddenly he had a thought. He put on his coat and hat and went into the front room. From the window he could see the policeman passing the house. He waited, and held his breath.

After a few moments he went out of the house, shutting the door very gently behind him. Then he began ringing the bell. In about five minutes a servant appeared. He was half dressed and looked very sleepy.

'I am sorry I had to wake you up, Francis,' he said, stepping in. 'But I have forgotten my key. What time is it?'

'Ten minutes past two, sir,' answered the man, looking at a clock.

'Ten minutes past two? How horribly late! You must wake me at nine tomorrow. I have some work to do.'

'All right, sir.'

'Did anyone call this evening?'

'Mr Hallward, sir. He stayed here until eleven, and then he went away to catch his train.'

'Oh! I am sorry I didn't see him. Did he leave any message?'

'No, sir. He said he would write to you from Paris.'

'That is all, Francis. Don't forget to call me at nine tomorrow.'

'No, sir.'

The man went off to his bedroom.

Dorian Gray threw his hat and coat upon the table and passed into the library. For a quarter of an hour he walked up and down the room, biting his lip and thinking. Then he took down a book from one of the cupboards, and began to turn the pages. 'Alan Campbell, 152 Hertford Street, Mayfair.' Yes, that was the man he wanted.

Chapter 11   The Problem of the Body

At nine o'clock the next morning his servant came in with a cup of chocolate, and opened the curtains. Dorian was sleeping quite peacefully, lying with one hand under his cheek.

As he opened his eyes a smile passed across his lips. He turned round, and began to drink his chocolate. The November sun came into the room, and the sky was bright. It was almost like a morning in May.

Slowly he remembered what had happened the night before. The dead man was still sitting there, and in the sunlight now. How horrible that was! Such terrible things were for the darkness, not the day.

After he had drunk his cup of chocolate, he went over to the table and wrote two letters. One he put in his pocket, and the other he handed to his servant.

'Take this round to 152 Hertford Street, Francis. If Mr Campbell is out of town, get his address.'

When the servant had gone, he lit a cigarette, and began drawing on a piece of paper. First he drew flowers, then houses, then human faces. Suddenly he realized that every face he drew looked like Basil Hallward. He frowned and went over to lie on the sofa.

An hour went past very slowly. Every second he kept looking up at the clock. As the minutes went by he became horribly worried. He got up and walked around the room. His hands were strangely cold.

At last the door opened, and his servant entered.

'Mr Campbell, sir,' said the man.

The colour came back to his cheeks.

'Ask him to come in at once, Francis.' He felt himself again. His fear had gone away.

In a few moments Alan Campbell walked in. He looked very angry and rather worried.

'Alan! This is kind of you. I thank you for coming.'

'I hoped never to enter your house again, Gray. But you said it was a question of life and death.' His voice was hard and cold, and he kept his hands in the pockets of his coat.

'Yes, it is a question of life and death, Alan. And to more than one person. Sit down.'

Campbell took a chair by the table, and Dorian sat opposite him. The two men's eyes met. In Dorian's there was great sadness. He knew that what he was going to do was terrible.

After a moment of silence, Dorian said very quietly, 'Alan, in a locked room at the top of the house, a dead man is sitting at a table. He has been dead for ten hours now. Don't stir, and don't look at me like that. You don't need to know who this man is. You don't need to know how or why he died. What you have to do is this –'

'Stop, Gray. I don't want to know anything more. I don't care if what you tell me is true or not true. I don't want any part in your life. Keep your horrible secrets to yourself. They don't interest me any more.'

'Alan, they will have to interest you. I am awfully sorry for you, Alan. But I can't help myself. You are the one man who can save me. Alan, you are a scientist. You know about chemistry, and things of that kind. What you have got to do is to destroy the thing that is upstairs.'

'You are mad, Dorian. I will have nothing to do with this.'

'He killed himself, Alan.'

'I am glad of that. But who made him do it? You, I suppose.'

'Do you still refuse to do this for me?'

'Of course I refuse. You have come to the wrong man. Go to some of your friends. Don't come to me.'

'Alan, it was murder. I killed him. You don't know what he made me suffer.'

'Murder! Good God, Dorian, is that what you have come to? I will have nothing to do with it.'

'You must have something to do with it. Don't ask any more questions. I have told you too much already. But you must do this. We were friends once, Alan.'

'Don't speak of those days, Dorian. They are dead.'

'They will hang me for this, Alan. Don't you understand? They will kill me for what I have done.'

Campbell got up to leave. 'I will not have anything to do with this.'

'You refuse?'

'Yes.'

The same look of sadness came into Dorian Gray's eyes. Then he took a piece of paper and wrote something on it. He read it over and pushed it across the table. Then he got up and went over to the window.

Campbell looked at him in surprise and picked up the paper. As he read it, his face went white, and he fell back in his chair.

After two or three minutes without speaking, Dorian came and stood next to him.

'I am very sorry for you, Alan,' he said, putting his hand on his shoulder. 'But there is no other way. I have a letter written already. Here it is. You see the address. If you don't help me, I will send it. You know what will happen. But you are going to help me. It is impossible for you to refuse now.'

Campbell put his face in his hands.

'The thing is quite simple, Alan. It has to be done. Face it, and do it.'

A terrible sound came from Campbell's lips.

'Come, Alan, you must decide now.'

Alan paused for a moment. 'Is there a fire in the room upstairs?'

'Yes, there is a gas fire.'

'I must go home and get some . . . things.'

'No, Alan, you must not leave the house. Write out what you want, and my servant will get the things for you.'

It was nearly two o'clock when the servant returned with an enormous wooden box filled with the things Campbell had asked for.

'You can have the rest of the day to yourself, Francis.'

'Thank you, sir.'

When the servant had left, the two men carried the box up the stairs. Dorian took out the key and turned it in the lock. Then he stopped and Campbell saw that his eyes were full of tears. 'I don't think I can go in, Alan,' he said.

'I don't need you,' said Campbell coldly.

Dorian half opened the door. As he did so, he saw the face of the portrait staring in the sunlight. He remembered that the night before he had forgotten to cover the picture. He was about to rush forward when he saw something that made him jump back.

There was blood on one of the hands in the portrait. How horrible it was!

He hurried into the room, trying not to look at the dead man. Picking the curtain off the floor he threw it over the picture. Then he rushed out of the room and down the stairs.

It was long after seven when Campbell came back into the library. He was quiet and white in the face, but very calm. 'I have done what you asked me to do,' he said. 'And now goodbye. Let us never see each other again.'

'You have saved me, Alan. I cannot forget that,' said Dorian, simply.

When Campbell had left he went upstairs. There was a horrible smell in the room. But the thing that had been sitting at the table was gone.

Chapter 12   'Why Do You Look so Young'

'Don't tell me that you are going to be good,' cried Lord Henry. 'You're quite perfect. Don't change.'

Dorian Gray shook his head. 'No, Harry, I have done too many terrible things in my life. I am not going to do any more. But tell me, what is happening here in London? I have been out of the country for more than a month.'

'People are still discussing poor Basil's disappearance.'

'Are they not bored with that yet?' said Dorian, pouring out some wine and frowning.

'My dear boy, they have only been talking about it for six weeks.

There was blood on one of the hands in the portrait.
How horrible it was!

The British only need one subject of conversation every three months. They have been very lucky recently, though. First there was the scandal of my wife leaving me, and then Alan Campbell killed himself. Now there is the mysterious disappearance of an artist. The British police are saying that Basil did take the midnight train on the ninth of November, but the French police are sure that he never arrived in Paris at all.'

'What do you think has happened to Basil?' asked Dorian, holding up his wine against the light.

'I have no idea. If Basil wants to hide himself, it is no business of mine. If he is dead, I don't want to think about him. Death is the only thing that ever frightens me. I hate it.'

'Why?' said the younger man, in a tired voice.

'Because,' said Lord Henry, 'it is the only thing that is final. Let us have our coffee in the music room, Dorian. You must play Chopin to me. The man who ran away with my wife played Chopin beautifully. Poor Victoria! I was very fond of her. The house is quite lonely without her.'

Dorian said nothing, but went into the next room and sat at the piano. After the coffee had been brought in, he stopped playing.

'Harry,' he said, looking over at Lord Henry. 'Do you think Basil was murdered?'

Lord Henry yawned. 'Everyone liked Basil. Who would want to murder him? He was not clever enough to have enemies. Of course he was a wonderful painter. But a man can paint like Velasquez and yet still be rather boring. Basil was really rather boring. The only thing that interested me about him was that he worshipped you.'

'I was very fond of Basil,' said Dorian sadly. 'But don't people say he was murdered?'

'Oh, some newspapers do. But I don't think it is likely. I know there are awful places in Paris, but Basil was not the sort of man to go to them.'

'What would you say, Harry, if I told you that I had murdered

Basil?' said the younger man. He watched him carefully after he had spoken.

'No, Dorian, you would not murder anyone. It is ordinary people who murder. It is their way of finding the extraordinary pleasure that art gives us.'

'A way of finding the extraordinary pleasure? Do you think that a man who has murdered could do it again. Don't tell me that.'

'Oh! Anything becomes a pleasure if you do it too often,' cried Lord Henry, laughing. 'That is one of the most important secrets of life. I believe, though, that murder is always a mistake. One should never do anything one cannot talk about after dinner. But let us pass from poor Basil. I wish I could believe that he has died some romantic death, but I can't. He probably fell into the Seine off a bus. I can see him now lying on his back in the dirty green water. During the last ten years he had not been painting well.'

Lord Henry walked across the room and touched the head of a strange grey bird that he kept in the music room. Then he turned to face Dorian.

'Yes,' he continued, taking his handkerchief out of his pocket, 'his painting seemed to me to have lost something. When you and he stopped being great friends, he stopped being a great artist. What was it that separated you? I suppose he bored you. If so, he never forgave you. By the way, what happened to that wonderful portrait he did of you? I don't think I have ever seen it since he finished it.'

'I told you years ago that it was stolen.'

'Oh! I remember. You never got it back? What a shame! It really was wonderful. I remember I wanted to buy it. I wish I had it now.'

'I never really liked it,' said Dorian. 'I am sorry I sat for it. The memory of the thing is hateful to me.'

'How sad you look! Don't be so serious. Play me some music, Dorian. And, as you play, tell me in a low voice why you still look so young. I am only ten years older than you are, and I have grey hair and yellow skin. You are really wonderful, Dorian.'

'Harry, please –'

'You have never looked more charming than you do tonight. You remind me of the day I first saw you. You were very shy, and absolutely extraordinary. You have changed, of course, but not in appearance. You are still the same.'

'I am not the same, Harry.'

'Yes, you are the same. I wish I could change places with you, Dorian. The world has cried out against us both, but it has always worshipped you. It always will worship you. Life has been your art.'

Dorian got up from the piano, and passed his hand through his hair. 'Yes, life has been beautiful,' he said, quietly, 'but I am not going to have the same life, Harry. And you must not say these things to me. You don't know everything about me. I think that if you did, even you would turn away from me. You laugh. Don't laugh.'

'Why have you stopped playing, Dorian? Let us go to the club. It has been a charming evening, and we must end it charmingly. There is someone I want to introduce to you – young Lord Poole. He has already copied your ties and he very much wants to meet you. He is quite charming and he reminds me of you.'

'I hope not,' said Dorian, with a sad look in his eyes. 'But I am tired tonight, Harry. I won't go to the club. It is nearly eleven, and I want to go to bed early.'

'Please stay. You have never played so well as tonight.'

'It is because I am going to be good,' he answered, smiling. 'I am a little changed already.'

'You can't change to me, Dorian,' said Lord Henry. 'You and I will always be friends. Come round tomorrow. We shall go to lunch.'

'Do you really want me to come, Harry?'

'Certainly. The park is quite lovely now. I don't think there have been such flowers since the year I met you.'

'Very well. I shall be here at eleven,' said Dorian. 'Good-night, Harry.'

Chapter 13 'To Kill the Past'

It was a lovely night. He walked home, with his coat on his arm, smoking his cigarette. Two young men in evening dress passed him. He heard one of them whisper to the other, 'That is Dorian Gray'. He remembered how pleased he used to be when he was stared at, or talked about. He was tired of hearing his own name now.

When he reached home, he found his servant waiting up for him. He sent him to bed, and threw himself down on the sofa in the library. He began to think about some of the things that Lord Henry had said to him.

Was it really true that one could never change? There had been a time when he had been good and innocent. He had corrupted himself, and become a terrible influence on others. He had even got pleasure from this corruption. Yet his soul had once been the purest of all. Was all that gone? Was there no hope for him?

In one terrible moment of passion, he had asked to stay young for all time. All his failure had been because of that. He had not been punished, but perhaps punishment was what he had needed. Punishment cleaned the soul.

The mirror that Lord Henry had given to him, so many years ago now, was standing on the table. He picked it up, remembering that horrible night when he had first noticed the change in the picture. Once, someone who had loved him passionately had written him a mad letter. It had ended with these words: 'The world is changed because you are made of gold.' He repeated them to himself and suddenly realized that he hated his own beauty. Throwing the mirror on the floor, he broke the glass into little pieces with his foot. It was his beauty that had spoiled him.

It was better not to think of the past. Nothing could change that. He had to think of his future. Alan Campbell had shot himself one night, and his terrible secret had died with him. The interest in Basil Hallward's disappearance would soon pass away. He was perfectly safe there.

What worried him was the death of his own soul. Basil had painted the portrait that had destroyed his life. He could not forgive him that. It was the portrait that had done everything. The murder had just been the madness of the moment. As for Alan Campbell, he had killed himself. It was nothing to do with Dorian Gray.

A new life! That was what he wanted. That was what he was waiting for. Perhaps it had begun already. He would never again spoil innocence. He would be good.

He began to wonder if the portrait in the locked room had changed. Was it still as horrible as it had been? Perhaps if his life became pure, the face in the portrait would become beautiful again. He would go and look.

He took the lamp from the table and went upstairs. As he opened the door, a smile of happiness passed across his young face. Yes, he would be good, and the ugly thing he had locked away would not frighten him any more. He felt happier already.

He went in quietly, locking the door behind him. Walking straight over to the portrait, he took off the purple curtain that was covering it. An angry cry of pain came from him. He could see no change. The thing was still hateful – more hateful, even, than before. The red mark on the hand seemed brighter and more like new blood. And why was the red mark larger than it had been? It was all over the fingers now. There was blood on the painted feet, and blood on the hand that had not held the knife.

What did it all mean? That he should go to the police? That he should tell the whole story, and be put to death? He laughed. He felt the idea was absurd. If he did tell them now, who would believe him? There was nothing left of the murdered man anywhere. He had destroyed everything belonging to Basil Hallward. He himself had burned the bag and the coat. They would simply say he was mad.

Was this murder to follow him all his life? Was he always going to suffer because of his past? Yet what could he do? Go to the police? Never.

There was only one thing they could use against him and that was the picture itself. He would destroy it. Why had he kept it so long? Once it had given him pleasure to watch it changing and growing old. Recently he had felt no such pleasure. It had kept him awake at night. When he had been away, he had been frightened that another person would see it. Just the memory of it spoiled many moments of happiness. He would destroy it.

He looked around and saw the knife that had killed Basil Hallward. He had cleaned it many times until there was no mark left on it. It was bright, and it shone. It had killed the painter. Now it would kill the painter's work, and all that it meant. It would kill the past. When that was dead he would be free. He picked up the knife and pushed it into the picture.

There was a cry, and a crash. The cry was so horrible that frightened servants woke and came out of their rooms. Two gentlemen, who were passing in the Square below, stopped, and looked up at the great house. They hurried on until they met a policeman, and brought him back. The policeman rang the bell several times, but there was no answer. Except for a light in one of the top windows, the house was all dark. After a time, he went away and stood in the garden of the next house and watched.

'Whose house is that?' asked the older of the two gentlemen.

'Mr Dorian Gray's, sir,' answered the policeman.

They looked at each other as they walked away, and laughed cruelly. They knew who Dorian Gray was.

Inside the house the servants were talking in low whispers to each other. Old Mrs Leaf was crying. Francis was as white as death.

Lying on the floor was a dead man in evening dress. He had a knife in his heart.

After about a quarter of an hour, they went fearfully upstairs. They knocked, but there was no reply. They called out. Everything was still. They tried the door. It was locked. Finally, they got on the roof and came into the room through the window.

When they entered the room they found a portrait hanging on the wall. It showed Mr Dorian Gray as they had last seen him, young and beautiful. Lying on the floor was a dead man in evening dress. He had a knife in his heart. He was old and horribly ugly. It was not until they saw his rings that they recognized who the man was.

ACTIVITIES

Chapters 1–3

Before you read

1 Look at the pictures in this book. Do you think the story takes place:
   a now?
   b fifty years ago?
   c 100 years ago?

2 These words come in this part of the story. Use a dictionary to learn their meaning.

   exhibit   extraordinarily   flatter   frown
   passion   portrait   soul   worship

   Find the right meaning for each word.
   a very strong feelings like love and anger
   b to put on a show
   c a painting of a person
   d the part of a person that lives after death
   e to have a cross look on one's face
   f unusually
   g to say nice things (not always true!) to someone
   h to love someone completely

3 Learn the meaning of these words. Then write sentences with the words to show their meaning.
   a fascinating
   b charming
   c influence

After you read

4 Answer these questions:
   a What are Basil Hallward's feelings for Dorian Gray?
   b What are Dorian Gray's feelings for Basil?
   c What wish does Dorian make when he sees the finished portrait?
   d In Chapter 3, who has Dorian fallen in love with?
   e Lord Henry receives a telegram. What information does it contain?

5 What does Lord Henry mean when he says 'some little actress'?

Chapters 4–6

Before you read

6 These words come in this part of the story. Use a dictionary to learn their meaning.

absurd scandal tragedy

Find the right meaning for each word:

a a situation which is very sad

b a situation which shocks people

c very silly

7 Do you think that Dorian and Sybil will really get married? Discuss this with other students.

After you read

8 'I don't want to be an actress any more.'

a Why has Sybil changed her mind about acting?

b What effect does this have on Dorian?

c How does this cause a tragedy?

9 'The portrait was going to carry his shame.' (Chapter 6) What does this mean?

10 Dorian doesn't think he is heartless. What do you think? Discuss this with other students.

Chapters 7–8

Before you read

11 To be *corrupted* means:

a to become better

b to become bad

c to become important

12 Look at the picture on page 35. What do you think Basil is saying? And what is Dorian saying?

After you read

13 'You will sit for me again?' (page 38)

    a What does Basil mean by this question?

    b Why does Dorian refuse?

14 Describe how Dorian arranges to hide the portrait.

Chapters 9–10

Before you read

15 Dorian has decided to hide the portrait. Do you think any of the other people in the story will be allowed to see it? If so, who? Discuss your views with other students.

After you read

16 Why does Basil come to see Dorian?

17 Who says these words? What does the speaker mean?

    a 'I will show you my soul. You will see what you think only God can see.'

    b 'Is this what you have done with your life?'

18 Why do you think that Dorian kills Basil?

Chapters 11–13

Before you read

19 Dorian needs to get rid of Basil's dead body. How can he do it? Discuss your ideas with other students.

After you read

20 At first, Alan Campbell refuses to do what Dorian wants. Why does he change his mind?

21 How does the portrait change after the death of Basil?

22 Describe what the servants find when they finally enter the room where the portrait is.

Writing

23 Sybil Vane was a beautiful and popular actress. Write a newspaper report of her death.

24 Lord Henry and Basil are both close friends of Dorian. How are their characters different? Which one do you prefer?

26 You are Dorian. You keep a diary. Write about the day when you arranged for Alan Campbell to get rid of Basil's body.

26 The changes in the portrait seem to happen by magic. Think of a story (perhaps a film) in which something magical happens. Tell the story.

27 Dorian seems to think that beauty is important and that kindness is not. Give three examples of his love of beauty and three examples of his lack of kindness.

28 Write a note to a friend, describing this book. Say if your friend will like it or not and why.

Answers for the activities in this book are available from your local
Pearson Education office or contact: Penguin Readers Marketing Department,
Pearson Education, Edinburgh Gate, Harlow, Essex, CM20 2JE.